A Journey Through Selves

Krystal Gervais

BookLeaf Publishing

India | USA | UK

Made with ❤ on the BookLeaf Publishing Platform
www.bookleafpub.in
www.bookleafpub.com

For Katharine Marie Bazile (Ma),

Who taught me how to dream, how to feel deeply,

and how to find beauty in the chaos.

Acknowledgments

This poetry book is a labor of love, a reflection of my journey, and a tribute to those who have shaped my life and supported my growth.

First and foremost, I dedicate this book to my beloved mother, Katharine Maric Bazile, whom I lovingly called Ma. Your spirit lives on in every word I write, and your love, strength, and lessons continue to guide me. Ours was a complex relationship, and though times were often difficult, I still found myself admiring you and learning from you. Your resilience, creativity, and the depth of your emotions have shaped so much of who I am. This book would not exist without the inspiration you provided and the resilience you instilled in me. I miss you deeply and carry you with me always.

To my maternal grandmother, Teodora Aguilar-Bazile, though our time together was brief, I still remember your love and adoration for me. Your care and warmth, even in those short years, left a profound impact on my heart that I carry to this day.

To my late Auntie Margarine, who taught me to see the humor in life and loved me like a mother. You were my saving grace growing up, always giving me the real—raw and uncut—while wrapping it in love and care. You were truly a trip without a suitcase, and your vibrant spirit continues to inspire me.

To my father, Steven Gervais, whose complexities and humanity have deeply influenced me. Despite the challenges we faced, I will always see the good in you and recognize the ways you shaped my character. Your openness to learning about others, even when grappling with the weight of a difficult upbringing, taught me the value of empathy and understanding. Thank you for showing me how to see the humanity in everyone.

To my stepmother, Nicole Atwood, who has shown me unconditional love and care, filling my life with the nurturing presence of a mother. I am eternally grateful for the way you have loved and supported me as your own.

To my maternal grandfather, Rev. Elvin J Bazile, whose consistent love and grace have been a foundation in my life. You have taught me to always be aware of my surroundings, to trust in God, and to approach life with integrity and faith. You have been a steady father figure to me, and I am endlessly thankful for your wisdom and presence. Your love and guidance will forever be cherished.

To my step-grandmother, Jerralyn Ambrose-Bazile, whose strength, resilience, and encouragement to "know thyself" have been invaluable. Your guidance has pushed me to explore deeper levels of self-awareness, and your support has left a lasting imprint on my soul.

To my paternal grandparents, Norman Gervais and especially my Maw-maw, Betty Gervais, who imparted the love and wisdom that only grandparents can offer. Your influence is a part of every page.

To my family, friends, and loved ones who have supported me through the highs and lows of my journey, I am endlessly grateful.

To Alimah, Terrie, Lindsey, and Stacy, thank you for teaching me about sisterhood and the complexities of sustaining relationships. Each of you, in your own way, has helped me understand the beauty and challenges of connection.

A special thank you to my spiritual guides, mentors, and the teachings and influences of Neville Goddard, Ram Dass, Nikki Giovanni, David Hawkins, Anandamayi Ma, Eckhart Tolle, Joseph Rodrigues, Maya Angelou, Gabor Maté, and so many others. Your wisdom has been a beacon of light, helping me navigate the complexities of life and inspiring me to live authentically and with purpose.

To Echo, my playful and comforting feline companion, your presence has brought light into my days. You remind me to find joy in the simple things.

To my readers: thank you for taking the time to immerse yourselves in my words. This book is as much for you as it is for me—a testament to the power of vulnerability, creativity, and connection. May these poems resonate with your heart and remind you of the beauty in both light and shadow.

Lastly, to Benny, whose wisdom and support have been a tremendous gift on this path. Your encouragement and unwavering belief in my abilities have meant more than words can express.

With gratitude and love,
Krystal Gervais

Preface

This collection is a dedication to the spirit of transformation and the unyielding beauty found in our darkest hours. It is for anyone who has ever felt misunderstood, broken, or disconnected, and yet, like me, continues to search for the light within the shadows. These poems are my love letter to growth, resilience, and the divine creativity that emerges when we allow ourselves to be vulnerable and whole.

My story is woven through these pages—the echoes of a childhood shaped by pain and tenderness, the rawness of grief after losing my mother, and the deep introspection that followed. As a poet, hairstylist, teacher, and dreamer, I have come to understand that art, like life, is not about perfection. It's about expression, about healing, and about connecting with the pieces of ourselves that we sometimes fear to confront.

For years, I silenced my voice, unsure of its worth. Writing these poems became my bridge to self-discovery and a reminder that even in our brokenness, we are worthy of love and understanding. I hope these words help you feel seen, validated, and reminded of the infinite potential within your soul.

This book is also a tribute to my mother, whose strength and spirit continue to inspire me, even in her absence. She taught me that beauty and resilience often reside in the same place and that creativity is one of the most sacred acts of self-love. I write these poems for her, for myself, and for you—the reader who dares to feel deeply and love unapologetically.

Thank you for holding space for my words. May this collection offer you the comfort of knowing that wherever you are on your journey, you are not alone.

With love and light,
Krystal Gervais

9/24/19

I'm still caught in some confusion
Feels like contusion
Feelings reside, but sliding around
Is it an illusion?
A fusion of my heart and mind?
Now that would draw the masses
Instead, emotional chaos-tsunami
Left wondering what the hell happened
Consistent inconsistencies
Your type of caretaking leaves me in a state of
disharmony
We don't understand each other at all
And I don't realize it 'til after the fall
I thought I needed you
But I don't need you at all
The windows to my soul are closed to all
involved
But you're not the bandit
You're not the "bad guy"
The one who left my heart bandaged
See, I came like that already
Thinking I was damaged
But really this is just a growth spurt

That for a second, I thought I couldn't
manage
"Saving Krystal" is the theme
Grandpa gave me that
I have to take care of myself first
Before helping those who lack
It would take a whole lot more from you
To be able to truly have me
You never really had me
Because I was never completely sure
If what we had was genuine
Or if little pieces were just picked up off the
floor
And given to me
Not much thought involved
Just fashioned yourself after what you saw
What you thought I wanted to see
So that when I look at you
I see me
But I don't recognize you.
Anymore.

DNS

A dark night of the soul
Can last as long as Truth
You may never find the way
Back through the mysteries of You

It feels like a drawn-out death
To which you would welcome if you could
Because sometimes feeling so alone
Isn't really understood

The tears start as droplets
And soon form a stream
Flows into River and Ocean
And back into Me

I squint as I continue on
Every now and then, sing out a song
In hopes of seeing some shape or form
Or a place where I belong

There's nowhere to hide
From myself
I will find

New ways to define
The perimeters of my mind

The tears start as droplets
And soon form a stream
Flows into River and Ocean
Right back into Me

Untitled

Well, I'm afflicted, too!
I used to have a passion, a sort of love that
Soared through my soul, but left me with
Sores through my soles.
My feet hurt
From this long journey of trial and error.
Why won't he pick me? Am I not pretty
enough?
Love is a funny thing, but it's hard to laugh
With all this hurt she brings
See, she tends to deceive me, and make me
Mistake hugs for trust
Shrugs for must, and eventually,
Love for lust.
Yeah, it's sad, but don't make me out to be
The center of your pity.
I don't want sympathy.
I just want simply a symphony
Symbolizing
Playing the tune of emancipation and
liberation.
I wanna be free from all these dudes and their
faking!

Might be one or two or a few that's real.
Might be one or two or a few that's sincere.
But it doesn't matter.
"Don't take me for granted; this is your last
chance!"
I tend to say that a lot
But fail to tell them I'm a pathological liar
"I love you, girl."
Yeah, I love you too
But in my mind, I'm playing the same games
you do.
And in playing these "Love Olympics"
I find more reason to doubt myself
And label myself NOT GOOD ENOUGH.
But you know, maybe it's not that
I'm not good enough...
Maybe I'm too good.
Maybe I'm a goddess in disguise
That these boys, these dogs, feel they
Can't treat right.
Not because I'm not good enough
But because they ain't worthy.
And they ain't worth ME.
But damn, if that's the case,

Then why does Love continually slap me in
the face?
I need space, I need time, I need faith!
'Cause I'm running real low right now,
My tank needs patience
And I need another roll of Standing Here
Waiting.
I hate love!
How can something so delicate, so soft
Twist my head off and misplace my mind?
How can she be so rough?
I don't get it.
Forget it.
But then again, I live it.

American BDSM

Lately I've been in the mood to be
blindfolded.
You know some kinky things can happen
when one is
Blindfolded.
I mean some mind-blowing, time-woven, hot
and steamy,
"Yes, please may I have another?" Blindfolded.
I like it rough.
I like how the government fucks.
How he leaves us taxpayers to clean up his
nut.
But he has good dick, though. $700 billion
worth.
Price tag might be big, but he's my first.
I mean, I want to be with him, but I know
there's someone else.
Afghanistan or Iraq...
What do they have that I lack?
Then you have the nerve to want to
impregnate them with American soldiers?
Wait, hold up.
Blindfold me. I can't bear to watch.

Bring your children home where they'll be
taken care of.
This ain't fair, Love...
Stop making me pay for everyone else's
bankruptcy.
You can be so good to me when you want to
be
But as soon as times get hard, you get up and
leave.
                              Blindfold me.
Fuck me harder. I'm getting used to it.
I'm starting to get the impression that you
don't know what to do with it!
Maybe if you gave me some head or
knowledge
Instead of all these spurts of corruption and
misjudgment
I might be satisfied.
And maybe I wouldn't act so ignorant and so
desperate.
I'm out of patience.
All I want are the simple things in life, like
free healthcare or a steady occupation.
You can barely take care of me;

How are you going to take care of someone
else's nation?
And I know I'm not your favorite
But you can't breathe without me.
You can't plant your seed without me, which
means
You can't mislead without me.
I'm your heartbeat, but you treat me like you
can sleep without me.
Times are hard right now.
My cashflow is dwindling and
My faith in you is weaker than it's ever been.
The fire that was sparked by the wealthy
needs some rekindling.
Hopefully in a good way that lasts for more
than the decades that we're living in.

        Blindfold me.
I hate watching the rich get richer
While the poor get poorer.
So many of these wealthy bigots only worry
about getting their status quo up.
I'm about to lose my house, man. Where you
been? Why you didn't show up?
I thought we were in this together

But you bailed out and failed.
And now you're buying up all these banks
that are for sale.
And guess who's stuck with the bill?
That would be me. Middle-class America
In the Land of the Free.
Where our government knows just how to
complicate things.
In a place where murder and poverty
dominate scenes.
Can shit get better? Probably.
Or will American blood continue to saturate
foreign soil?
Well, we'll have to see.

Unblindfold me

When it comes to be.

Some Blues 10/14/18

How to overcome overwhelming thoughts of
hurt?
Is this what it means to hover over earth?
What am I worth?
I know it's not your job to put me first
But I thought...
But I thought... More of the same.
Same brain.
What am I supposed to think?
On the brink.
In the kitchen sink. Wink.
Not your job to comfort me
But I really feel like I need comforting.
Damn. Am I strong enough to manage?
Damage done.
Theraflu Blues on the bayou.
Love enhances.
I know not what else to do but LOVE.
Same brain.
I give to please.
But what if it leaves me on my knees?
What am I supposed to think?
On the brink.

In the kitchen sink. Wink.
Not your job to comfort me
But I really need comforting.
Damn. Am I strong enough to manage?
Damage done.
Theraflu Blues on the bayou.
Love enhances.
I know not what else to do but LOVE.

Maintenance 7/26/16

Watching the sounds of the water take place
Feeling Earth's tears streaming down my face
Cars pass by one by one
Some leave a trail of squeaks
Shouts of pain from beneath metal frames.
Oil leak?

Week Ends Here 8/30/15

Sitting on a bench at the Lakefront
comfortably
Mind wandering
Blank stares
Food affairs happening at Landry's
Watching sailboats float away into the
distance
Funny how the smallest things make you
question your existence
This breeze feels so good dancing across my
face
Entangling my hair just enough
To give me an easy time detangling it
Hearing the banter of old friends
Or maybe new acquaintances
Surface conversations
With the background music
Of Hotboys', "The Block is Hot"
The smell of good weed ablaze.

Sun has set on this Sunday now
Everyone going back to their
Monday growl

Dreaming of next weekend...

Nothin' to Worry About
9/26/15

Sitting beneath the depths of my reflection,
Staring up at my beauty in amazement.
I can smell the placid waters
And they whisper in my ear
"No worries about your one true love,
because we'll always be right here."
I listen in contentment.
My heart makes a commitment
That no matter what this life may bring,
The Sun and Moon will sing this song to me:
"We will never leave your side.
   Listen to your voice inside.
   Love is infinite; it forms the sky
   So that Heaven's wings can help you fly."
In amazement, I wonder what else
could lie in the deep abyss of my soul?
As the Sun rises, so do I.
I watched as the night sky filled with stars I
was made in the image of
Fade into the light the Sun gifts. So generous.

Goodness and Resounding Yearnings

I yearn for a taste of which I know not.
The thirst of a girl staring at a fast-flowing
river.
She's known this river since antiquity.
She's slept on the river's bed,
Whether filled with ancient fragments
Or just sandy and flat.
Patience. Balance.
As she watched this river overflow its banks
and kiss the ground surrounding it
Joyfully,
She smiled back and planted her seeds.
At that moment I realized I needed that river
And that river needed me.
For too long, it had been used as a means of
adoration
Or transportation.
The time had come for it to fulfill a new
purpose.
I, then Egypt, awaited passionately for
this river to inundate my land year after year.

And year after year, those crops fed my
people.
My soul.
Those waters and I: whole.
One day, whilst swimming carefree,
Curiosity beckoned me
And I swam upstream.
To my surprise, I happen upon a dam.
Yet another great discovery to add more
Depth to this divine body of water!
Then disappointment consumed me.
I couldn't get through.
I had no choice but to climb
back over those banks and not with ease.
Perspiration and tears.
Forced to face fears.
Over time, with each dam encountered,
I became stronger.
I became the dam, the tributaries,
the bank (by which I had already gained a
fortune).
I became the pain of being used,
abandoned.
I became the bed, the water itself.

I lovingly observe that girl staring at the
fast-flowing river,
thirsting for those waters of which
she knows not the taste.
Feeling the need to possess something outside
of herself.
She will forever remain parched
Until she remembers that she is
The river.

Daddy's Little Girl
8/2/17

Fist fights with my father.
Alcohol. So much pain.
He punched me like I wasn't shit.
Pulled my hair.
I love him so much.
I'm so hurt.
Staring at my mother's ashes, wishing she was
here.
Pain. Tears.

Higher thinking?
Lesson in all of this?

TOO EMOTIONAL RIGHT NOW TO
SORT IT OUT.

Staring into the tin can, 1/4 full of my
mother's ashes.
My head hurts where he pulled my hair and
wouldn't let go.
I wonder if he pulled any out?

Tears.
Scratch on my face.
Pain.
My heart hurts.

Love's Cage 3/22/17

Once upon a time, there was a bird who lived wild and free. One day, she was captured by a being wearing a mask—disguised as Love. This bird had never truly known what Love was, so she trusted the illusion, believing that Love would never harm her.

At first, Love admired her, telling her how beautiful she was and how extraordinary she could be—if only she changed. He suggested she color her feathers differently, promising that other birds would worship her for it.

Love thought he was helping her, teaching her that her freedom wasn't enough and that she needed to compromise parts of herself to be worthy of Love.

As time passed, the bird grew more and more despondent. Despite Love's flowery compliments and grand promises of a bright future, he never truly nurtured her. He didn't feed her properly or care for her needs. He wanted her beauty to intoxicate him, to fill a void in himself, but he didn't know how to cherish her spirit.

Other birds had lived in his cage before. They
had delighted briefly in his attention, in the
crumbs of affection and entertainment he
offered. But in time, they too had been
discarded—released, or perhaps brought to
ruin and buried somewhere out of sight.
This bird was different. Love gazed at her
endlessly, obsessed with her wild beauty, but
his obsession left her hollow. Deprived of the
freedom that had once sustained her, she
withered. Love watched her fade,
unaware—or unwilling to see—that she was
starving.
And so, she died in his cage, a beautiful
memory trapped in his mind, her spirit long
gone.

What It Do? 7/29/18

What is truth?
Is it different from reality?
Who says what reality really is?
Who would I even trust to know
something like that?

I'm allowing too much outside influence to
affect me.
I don't feel like my actions or words are my
own
sometimes. A lot of times.
I feel stuck.
As much as I want a beloved
or a partner or lover...
I just want to feel loved
and nurtured.
By whom?
By whoever shows themselves to be true?
But what is truth?
What is reality?

I said I would go to church today,
but the water was calling me.

So, here I am.

Tears. Is this self-pity?
Am I being too hard on myself?
Who am I really?

I feel like I'm...

Trying to just listen to the
water and see what it has to say.

I miss you, Mom.

Wutchue Want?

I am awoken by what awaits me
As much as I try to escape hard decisions
Indecisiveness is my prison
Mind rocks back and forth
South and North
When it rains, it pours
Smiles mask all the sores
Wanna soar
Wanna feel forever more

2/9/18

Why do I insist on smoking my brains out
knowing I'm already high?
I don't know.

But anyway
I need to stop being afraid of change.
It sounded and felt like this would be easy
when I first embarked on this journey of
reinventing myself. Becoming "awake" and
"tuned in." It's like my inner child is throwing
a fit, and I just keep trying to coddle her and
make her feel better by giving her whatever
she wants. Sugar. Weed. Sex. Relationships.
Isolation. No accountability. I keep wrestling
with whether or not I'm depressed or just
lacking self-discipline. I feel like it's so so hard
to break free from this cycle. Pattern. I can no
longer fear change. I know I need to
surrender and let go. Rebirth requires death.

10/28/17

Loving you is a prison.
My yearning for your touch is handcuffs.
Binding me to thoughts of you.
I can't operate properly.
You're not my property.
These are ancient tears
Cried by so many women before me
Sincerely wanting to be loved purely
For me.
Trying not to let this waiver my confidence.
Common is not common sense.
We drew a line.
Put up a fence.
I guess this is goodbye
Again, my friend.

Taken Aback

Why is it so hard to let someone or something go when it no longer serves you?

ILLUSION

This just brings me right back to the starting position
Which is myself

I've had enough of Me.
The Me that holds on to dead weight.
The Me that doesn't keep her word.
The Me that keeps looking for validation, love,
Compassion, empathy, and understanding
Outside of herself.
Here I am again.
Burned. Strangled. Paralyzed
By just the hope of Love.
Handcuffed by my own expectations.
As I stand at this threshold once again
Feelings hurt. Tail between my legs...

I am almost still in disbelief that he could say
"Fuck u"
So freely in a text.
I'm not really sure if the feeling I'm
experiencing is a lesson
That my heart is using as a barbell to become
stronger
Or if this feeling is actually my heart slowly
becoming petrified;
Hardened by the injustices of Love.

Rejoice

As I close my eyes, I rewind Time
Infinite waters flowing through mind's eye
Thoughts are fluid
Rejoice through music
For the hard times
and the soft times

We be off at times
But what is Time, really?
The more important thing is that you feel me

And try to remember
To be thankful for Life's lessons
For they tend to morph into blessings

Try not to question too much
But at the same time, question everything
And if you find that Life is too rough
Just know that that's the Devil meddling

And we all gon' have to die first before we get
to Heaven
Sometimes you gotta be destroyed

To get put back together.
Rejoice.

New Poem

fear is an illusion
but it's hard to look away
when you're alone
forced to stare your insecurities in the face
I'm working on myself right now
what is progress?
I feel like the definition changes every day
but all finite things are subject to change,
right?
So, I arrange, trip over shit, then rearrange
Questioning if I'm crazy...
Am I like my mother? If so, in what ways?
I know at times I can be irrational
but it's my passion for life that makes small
issues seem impassable
what is fear?
an emotion induced by a threat perceived...
meaning
something that hasn't happened yet
like when you're living inside of an imagined
fence
Won't let nothing in, just in case of an
accident

'Cause your heart's been broken times before
and still, the cracks exist
I'm craving the very things I'm afraid of.

3 AM Blues

There's a knock at my door
Who could that be
Had just checked the time
Quarter to three
Don't want to get out of bed
But I guess I'll see
Who's decided, at this hour,
To come visit with me
Hard to get up, though
To get on my feet
I got this heavy heart
That's filled with defeat
And a mind full of thoughts
I'm ready to flee
To a place less familiar
To an unfamiliar me
I drag my feet
To the door
Open slowly
Cold, hard floor
Windy outside; forever more?
Nah, it's just me
With this cold, hard core

I see nobody here
I guess that's my clue
My loneliness came knocking
Its color, blue.

Adventure Time 11/16/15

once upon a time
        there was a girl looking
       for fantasies
searching in shallow water
      what could be
              found in only
     deeper seas
so sometimes she would
      light up the blunt
      to get her
            mind right

now

I Went Through Your Phone Last Night

While everyone was in a slumber
And my thoughts began to roam
I crept toward the sweet unknown
And tiptoed through your phone

I kept waking up through the night
With urges to release
But my mind was hijacked every time
So I had to find my peace

At the time I thought my peace would be
To roam free through your phone
Even though I was trying to find someone else
there,
My heart hoped no one was home

Then why go through the trouble?
Why hurt myself to no avail?
You wouldn't dare break my tender heart
Sealing my coffin with nails

No one was home last night
I breathed a sigh of relief
Only to wake up today with guilt
Laying heavily on top of me

My fear still runs rampant
But I vowed to tell the truth
I went through your phone last night
And there's really no excuse

12/25/21

I'm resting on a fallen Black Walnut tree
Thinking about things
Mind aimlessly wandering
In the dark, searching for a spark
Feeling an urge to cry
Exploring why
Is it my father?
Is it a yearning for things outside?
My awareness goes sometimes,
Or a lot of times
To bleak thoughts
I just want to let go and use everything I've
been taught
But the loopty loop must be fun to my ego
Wherever it wants to frolic
To the location, we go
Emotions, places, or people

Letting Go

My latest endeavor to be "better"
Will Life's tension ever let up?
Going with the flow, just to
Get up
Still questioning the moves I make
Give and take
Just an illusion
Body and mind, part of the contusion
I AM. That is all.
The rest is mere confusion
Practicing the letting go of Ego
Won't it loosen?
Don't mean to control others
Don't mean to manipulate
Don't want to be a mother
Except to those who are
Made out of my conception
Biological or impression
I want to love from the Divine
Don't wanna keep measuring love
By what's mine
Too much time to spend
Wanderin' in a place no one

Can find
A place where Ego dwells from behind
The veil
I cannot fail
I cannot mess up what's
For me
Wind in my sails
I always prevail
Gotta end my poems with faith
Gotta merge with Infinite
And know my heart is all it takes
My intention is the guide
To manifesting all my dreams
And if I die before it's real
That I forgot what it all means
Just wanna live a life of joy
Mixed with eternal peace
Everyday Life has new meaning
Everyday learning to Be

Happy Birthday

2/11

5:37

Happy to just be alive; I survived

I'm betrothed to my life

Yeah, my soul has arrived

Am I old? That's a tripe!

Ill-conceived notion in motion

Suppose to be right?

Am I right?

Yeah, alright

Attached to time

Attached to mind

You are your thoughts and your own design

And when you sleep you're intertwined.

Your innermost beliefs combined

But we forget before we remember...

A product of the Divine

Gardenia

Double chin, double chin
Big cheeks to hold bubbles in
Somethin' to store all knick-knacks
Kit-Kats and some Double Mint
I chose to eat them butter grits
I chose to keep on guzzlin'
Fuck it, I eat whenever I feel
Emotions get to bubblin'
But is it really me though?
Or
Is it rigid people?
Lookin' way too hard
At a body that can see you
I can see your hurt
Running miles inside your steeple
Judging eyes with crooked smiles
Tired and deceitful

Take a breath.

And in that space
Out from the depths
To in this case

Grows compassion
Into a flower that we
Both can embrace.

12/10/2020 7:30 am

I stare at the California sunset.
Unrest.
Unmanifested dreams unto my conscience.
Unemployed.
A little annoyed.
I'm an android
Unfit to exist
On this plane, I admit.
Unhinged.
Feelin' a little more distant tension
From my friends.
And in this instance
This Jameson hittin'
Is Prophet.
Hail to Almighty.
I'm unavailable, fighting.
My left wing won't submit to what's in
righting (writing)
And so my mind resorts to rioting.
It's tiring.
My threads have run real low.
I guess I have to do more tithing.
And in the meantime, mind me.

And if you got more questions then please
Leave a smiley
At the end of your expressions because
My senses tend to try me.
Sensitivity is a thing.
I'm workin' on my remedy.

A Danger to Self and Others

Mary Jane Essence
Used to wake up to a Backwood for breakfast
In and out of my death shit
Wanderin'
But I think I'm done again...?
Meditate in my sanctum
I will thank you
Repent to Higher Power and then I'll thank
you
I'm not ashamed to
I used to throw these daggers of Blame
And I had aim, Boo.

Ramblings

A quiet storm is raging within
My deepest feelings need a place to exist
Tried to ignore or deny but I quit
Because I no longer wish death on the
Light I emit

Come now, come all
I rise when I fall
See me with rose-colored glasses
Or see me in black
I am that
I Am.

No one reads captions
No longer the trend
Ingest my content
But not to the end
No time to waste
Yet no time to spend
A trip without a suitcase
To escape the Within.

Actually laughing
At my duality.
A casualty
With a not-so-casual
Sense of imagining.

I'll kill a thought before it kills me first
Lay in the dirt
I am in search
Of a fleeting feeling
Something unrehearsed
But alas
An old belief
Is deluding me with my past
Meeting
Dealing
Beating
Being

Chillin' in your sweats
Doin' reps
Of the weed
Filled with seeds
In the depths

Of distress
Whenever stressed
Puff for relief
I'm in debt
Like a pet
That I'll go get
To fill my needs
'Cuz I forget
That I meet death
Each time I quest
For what's underneath
I'm a seed
That's been planted
In the planet
I'm a tree.

I feel sad
I feel unease
I feel my throat tightening
Lighting in the breeze
I feel pain
I feel annoyed
I feel an aching
In my chest full of toys
I feel unseen

I feel unheard
I feel the agony of not knowing
What I'm worth
But haven't you heard?
It's always like this
The clock likes to tock
But mostly like to tick
And one day I'll return to a place from before
Frolic in my inner peace
Just have to find the door
Settled score
More of more

It's So Hard to Say Goodbye to Yesterday

Saying goodbye is never easy to do
Especially when someone's become part of
you
Having felt the flames of ecstasy and elation
turn cold blue
You question whether what you built together
was true
I choose to believe that love could never be
Contained, packaged, or renamed
It doesn't expire or have instructions on how
to maintain
It spontaneously exists with and without pain
It challenges us to grow out of concrete or
Through a drain
It's so inspiring, we sometimes become
blinded
And feel oppression
Admiration to obsession
Sinless to confession
Yearning to be free but bind ourselves
Learning as we teach and find ourselves

And lose one another in all the mayhem
Love is mindless yet humans construct a
playpen
Made out of time and endless thoughts of
past and future
Cover our scrapes and wounds with
All-consuming sutures
Ego-driven numbing for a starving ghost
I've turned into a shadow of what I loved
most
Because just the thought of love
turns into a post
About the thought of love
below a picture of a quote
About the thought of love
in hopes of getting some virtual gropes
From fellow provoked observers of Life's
Paradoxical show
The more I want love, it slows
The more we release love, it grows
The more we squeeze, hug with forced
affection and attention
It chokes
So let it go
Let the rhythm of God/Universe take full

control
Whatever that looks like will be different for
each
But the feeling of freedom and acceptance
Are sure to bring peace

To Catch a Predator (Thought)

Ooooooo look how sneaky
How sly
How insidious
Ooooooo look how creepy
How jive
How mischievous
Now, you been watchin' my every movement
My every attempt at improvement
But you sliiiiiiide your way into the essence
That I think is me
Dammmmmn that's some crazy shit, huh?
That the moment I elevate
You seem to elevate too
You learn the lingo and twist my words
against me
Constricting
Yet prolific
Convincing
That I am not whoever I say I am
Eminem voice
"If I wasn't then why would I say I am?

In my circle, crew every day I dance.
Radio station playin' the same ol' jams"
Let me roll a blunt right quick to lessen this
trick
Let me drink some gin right quick to deafen
this hit
Let me call ol' boy up to treat me like shit
So I distract these thoughts and project them
on him
I ain't gon' hold you
The way you finesse me to believe that the
worst
Parts of myself prove me unloveable
Is brilliant
gasps Think of the children!
Think of how many people you've been able
to build in
I think I can't
so I won't
I think I'm bad
so I'm alone
I'ma name you Fuzzy
'Cuz you comfort me in a sort of distorted
and
subtle way

But just enough to throw me off pace

Throw me off the Path
To a higher self that
I dream and get a glimpse of now and then
That state of mind that empowers me to first
Be my own best friend
Fuzzy, you make me nervous about ever
wantin' to
Try new shit again
My dude you out here wildin'
But I love your cringe
It is you, not me that's so scared to be alone
It is you, not me that's too scared of being
shown
My light through others
And it's ok 'cuz we goin' home
And we are safe so don't you groan
I don't want to kill you anymore
Or fight for this body
We ain't gotta go back and forth
'Til exhausted and groggy
We are but two peas in a pod
Way older than time
Fragmented at one point

And in another moment, sublime
So every time you stick your head out
Talkin' 'bout "I got you!"
I point my finger guns in your direction and
laugh
'Cuz it's not true

I Unfold

I unfold like a rose opening itself to the Sun
I unfold like an onion, various layers one by
one
I unfold like a shirt, creased and tucked away
I unfold like a $20 bill, stashed and forgotten
I unfold like a bathroom baby changing
station
I unfold like a piece of turkey bacon
I unfold like hooded eyes closed
I unfold like a favorite blanket
I unfold like a yoga pose
I unfold like Yoda
I unfold like the plot of a captivating story
I unfold like history repeats itself
I unfold like a dark night of the soul
Behold
I unfold like the rhythm of a jazz trio
I unfold like a chair
I unfold into something I don't even
recognize
I unfold and the light is so blinding and scary
That I contort myself back into the familiar
fold

Creases still intact, although less crispy
Not crispy enough to forget what I used to be
It feels good to go back into my drawer
I think I feel safe here

New Phone Who Dis?

Got a couple choices.
Retreat in defeat
Or stand on my square.
Never fear.
Rejection
Is my Everclear.
Pull me outta freeze state.
Bear witness to the weather cleared.
It's every year I reach out from my slumber.
In the depths of Life's wonders
With a depression pulling me under.
I'm like lightning's thunder.
Delayed a little bit, but I'm still a stunner.
Just please don't run from her.
Do I even exist if my sound doesn't have ears
to hear?

And it Hit Me Outta Left Field, Thought I had a Home Run, But I was just Getting Dugout

Tired of hearing how difficult I am to be with
You'll take me in my pieces
But never as a whole
Want me as a fragment
Afraid to see my soul
Destructive when we're together
Productive when apart
This played out so differently
Than how I saw
Our lives intertwined at just the right time
And unknotted slowly, piece by piece
Said our peace
Whatever that means
I mean it this time, though
Like many times before
When I was so hopeful
That things would be different

That I would be different
That you would still love me when I'm weak
That you would be different
And I would still love you when you didn't
speak
Now your silence is torture
And the words you do drum up
Stabs my already bleeding heart
Just leave me be
Say you want peace but bring war
Relationship stinks of disease
No more
Lay it to rest.

Lay it to Rest

The war is over
Sky no longer red with flames burning off
Accusations and screams of feeling
Misunderstood.
We did good.
We did all we could do.
Tomorrow will be a new day.
The sun will rise once again.
Yes, it will be a little different.
No more "Can I trust him?"
No more "Why did she betray me
Again?"
Just Life living itself.
I hope we can forgive ourselves for
Doing or saying things out of fear instead of
Love.
I hope the drug of Anxious and Avoidant
Attachment wears off with grace.
Sometimes the best we can do isn't enough to
Sustain a ship that wasn't built with the best
Materials.
A ship constantly on turbulent waters
With leaks bandaged by dreams of "what ifs".

I'm not afraid anymore.
I may have made mistakes but they don't
define
Who I am.
I'm much more than you give me credit for.
I've touched the depths of hell and came back
To live and love again.
I've touched the heavens only to be humbled
And learn to appreciate the little things.
You may not recognize me
But I am your reflection.
When you dream and see me again
I hope you flash me a smile
So I can see your glowing face and know
you're ok.
I hope Happiness and Peace and Love engulf
you
Like a comforting, warm blanket on a cold,
unbearable night.
And you might not believe me
Or my experiences to be true
But one thing I know for certain is
The great Love I have for you.

I've Given All I Could Give

Took missteps along the way
I did the best I could do with the perception I
had
At the time
I thought you could forgive me
I thought you would
And I just feel so misunderstood
But can't tell you that because, according to
you, I'm being
Manipulative
Hold the mirror closer to me
So I can see myself a little better
I'll pick through the debris and burnt
remnants
And still be able to see perfect imperfections
I'll continue to open my heart
And unfold
I'll live to see another day
And move with the lessons I've learned in tow
You go, be great
Go and experience experiences

I'll always love you
And parts of me will be with you always
In a sentimental mood
But at least I'm growing more and more
Understanding of myself

Baby, It's Cold Outside

It gets frigid when you go distant
Feels like death and I wish it didn't
This is the part I dread
When I just want to know what's going on so
Maybe I can help or just be
It is what it isn't
We're no longer children, able to ignore all
the
Outside noise and be in the moment
We've grown like weeds and you've got two
seeds
Who depend on your existence
I wish you wouldn't leave me out to freeze
I could see my breath out here
Outside of your heart
Please send me a signal or a heartbeat
That there's still love here
I keep trying to leave but turn back
Because I feel that you really love me
What is this?
I can only describe it as
Cold
Distance

Maybe it's self-preservation
In my tears and hopelessness about the future
I once built and cherished
Out of our conversations, hopes, and dreams
You have to travel on your own path and live
on
Your own means
I can only hope to do the same
And whenever I think of you I'll shed less and
Less tears
I'll keep remembering to be happy for you
And send you love
And just be so honored to have
Spent this time I got to spend with you
I try to reach out for your ghost
Although your body still lives
I'll still feel your soul...

Part II

One minute you want to devour me and feel
My essence on your tongue and remember
One minute I'm crying to just spend quality
time
One minute we're out eating
One minute you seem annoyed
Stressed out about money or having to spend
Money on me
Stressed out about not getting enough sleep
One minute you're telling me sleep doesn't
matter
And to come over whenever
One minute it's my fault you didn't get
enough sleep
One minute I long to be near you
One minute I block you and reserve to never
Speak to you again
One minute I just want to joke around
One minute I feel rejected and like
I'm somehow a nuisance
I don't want to feel like this anymore
I don't want an intricate web of a relationship
That I try so hard to navigate through and

map
And find ways to function that are
complementary
To both of us
Only for you to keep rearranging and tearing
down
Harmonizing with me one minute and
running away the next
It pains me to think of what you've been
through as a child
I try to show you so much love
But I slowly start to shut down
I don't feel I can be totally me
Isn't that reason enough to move on, Krystal?

How Dare You

How dare you come into my sanctum
Knowing you didn't want me fully.
Knowing how into you I've been.
You feel some type of way when people use
words
To gain one's trust for ill will
Is that not what you've done?
Didn't you know I'm a flower?
Don't you know I'm God?
Or did I confuse you by also being human?
I am Mother.
How dare you defile me.
You ingest my essence for your pleasure.
You consume me and savor the taste
Until the moment has passed
Like so many moments before.
How dare you constantly awaken my hope
For something different.
It's okay.
I have transformed and am still transforming
And you didn't have to do anything!
I yearn for you.
I obsessively think of you.

I want nothing more than to wash your taste
From my mouth
For good.
For the good of you and me.

Trauma Response

I love you
I need you
I breathe you
I see you
I'm open
I'm pure
I'm love
I'm yours
I'm kind
I'm nice
I'm flavor
I'm spice
I give and you take
You give and I break
Uncomfortable to receive,
I grieve
I cry
I hurt
Inside
I try
And try
To love you
To need you

Until I can't anymore
My heart overcome
From an unsettled score.

A Shoutout to the Ethers

If you ever got a chance to read my innermost
thoughts
And could actually and factually decipher
what I mean to say
Through the fog and through the murkiness
of my programming
What would you see?
What would there be?
Something you could hold on to and that you
could trust?
Something so innocent and forgiving that
Your heart would crack open
Like a pecan from Moonshine, La
See, I know where you come from
And your roots run so deep that they
Haphazardly run into my roots
Let that sink in
All this time I wanted you to know me
And at the same time show me
What you're made of
But now I know there's nothing to prove

Who am I?
There's nothing to do
But live the best way we could live
I am patient with you because
I'm learning to be patient with myself
And sometimes I need some help
And I call on you hoping you hear my
Whispering cry
I know at the end of the day I'm alone and
It's my choice whether I'm lonely
But I guess sometimes I could use some
Consoling
From the people I love
I'll figure it out that I'm figuring it out

Harriet the Spy

Stake out
Tryna get these shakes out
Wanting to know beyond a doubt
That it's me and only me you seek
But whilst trying to prove or refute my
Deepest fears
Somehow I lose myself in the process.
My Master Controls are overtaken.
Stomach in multiple knots.
Heart racing.
Now I have to defecate
But this shit's gotta stop.
How am I at the top of my game
When insecurities are allowed to pull me.
Drag me down.
Hoodied up with no drawers on
All stemming from one missed call.
"Well if only he would've answered,
Then maybe I wouldn't have to do all this."
Bullshit.
I do what I do because I am...
I am this human being that, as of late, has
been weighing

Life and death.
Waiting for a return to somewhere I haven't
found yet
My precious time right now could be spent
In meditation or making art or praying or
Drinking water or anything else besides
Having a stakeout.
Perpetuating darkness.
How am I supposed to harness
The good energy needed to elevate
If I keep leaping toward a downward slope?
How am I supposed to cope
When I don't even feel in control?
It's so old now
And I'm getting cold.
This has to be one of the saddest stories told.
Play the tiny violin for me.
Titanic's got a hole.
I'm sinking fast into the deep abyss
About to lose my soul.

HairPoetics

My hair is an extension of Me
Of who I choose to Be
It may change from week to week
As I change my mind to see
Myself more clearly

A Sleepy Sadness

Can't sleep
Mind rocking back and forth
In California peaks
Mountain high before I touch the sky
I'm envious of the mountain kissing the
clouds
The same way I want to kiss you
Elevated so much that the only space left to
fill
Is for our lips to touch
There's this eternal softness and gentleness
I've craved
You're this eternal softness and gentleness
I crave
But know not
I travel with my cross in tow
I'm a collection of scattered thoughts lost
In the corner store
Find my warm heart still beating next to the
Cold coffee
Gotta get this sadness off me.

Still

Really could care less about how the world
perceives me
Or how anyone reads me.
I'm not an open book so
You could judge me all you want.
I still won't break.
Still come around with a smile on my face.
A hypocrite is always among us.
A snake.
A liar.
A fake...
So fake that a desert wouldn't need rain
The clouds would make way
Just because the truth was being sprayed
But uh, other than that, you could make me
Out to be what you please.
I still won't cease.

1 Day as a Strugglin' Thug

I'm straight thuggin' it, ya heard me
My momma at home; she ain't worried
They could try, can't no one murk me
They want me but don't deserve me
I've been put under this curse, see
To where my anger just wanna burst free
My momma only first seed
So there ain't no need to choose who the
worst be
No matter how hard I try, I just can't help it
so I wonder
A thought that intrigues and even wakes me
from my slumber
Like, I'm the male tryna make things shake
with Life
But she gave me the wrong number
And as my heart grows number
I'm livin' envious
I'm way overdue for a switch
This Life's a bitch

Where is all this Blood Coming From?

On the street, you hear the sound of swift
feet.
Bullet shots fired, and I'm hit.
A flesh wound doesn't sound so bad once you
Find out you'll live. Sew it up and move on.
But where is all this blood coming from?

It's a sunny day as I feel the rays warm my
face.
For once, I don't see the crack in the sidewalk
and I trip.
A broken ankle doesn't sound so bad once
you
Find out you'll walk again. Wrap it up and
move on.
But where is all this blood coming from?

In the house now, sitting on the couch.
Raindrops fall and the lighting strikes hard.
A million volts of electricity doesn't sound so
bad once you

Find out you're not brain-fried. Live it up and
move on.
But where is all this blood coming from?

Despite what might happen to me
My heart will always bleed
With love for you
A rose that blooms
From the soul of just one seed.

I'm an Addict

Right now I'm on some other shit
Mind gone, I must admit
Call up them people, dial it quick
You call them police, I call them dicks

I took some drugs, took a lot
Mind gone, body hot
Some call it crack, some call it rock
I used to feel pain, but now I do not
Moved on to meth, I'm seeing things
Things that normal people don't see
I'm on Cloud 9 and I am free
And if you're wise, you'll get like me

Right now I'm on some other shit
Mind gone, I must admit
Call up them people, dial it quick
You call them police, I call them dicks

Hey, watch me as I hit the slopes
What I really mean is blow some coke
Can't handle Life, this helps me cope
All of my drugs give my life hope

I might be gay because I love this girl
She pleases me; she is my world
That Mary Jane makes my toes curl
If Life's a clam, then she's my pearl

Right now I'm on some other shit
Mind gone, I must admit
Call up them people, dial it quick
You call them police, I call them dicks

My day was shitty, need to forget
I don't care what, just need a fix
Promethazine I swallow quick
Contains no codeine? It ain't legit
No one knows about my habit
That I'm a fiend, that I'm an addict
Need no supplier 'cuz I have it
Cook it, bundle it, stash it, attack it

Right now I'm on some other shit
Mind gone, I must admit
Call up them people, dial it quick
You call them police, I call them dicks

So, my drugs have taken hold of me
They make me wise so I could see
They make me feel like I could be
A super hero or royalty
I might shoot up or snort a key
Smoke it down or swallow three
Some wonder how my piss stays clean
My drugs are actually Poetry

Safety First

I need to borrow someone's floaty
I'm about to be consumed by my own waves
of emotion
Despite the fact that it's up to me on how I
show them
I find myself not being able to control them
Some may hold them, but I lash out
My feelings build up and fly out my mouth
"Come back!"
But before I can grab them, they're already
involved in
Yet another homicide
Killing whoever so softly
Trespassing through their ears, entering their
innerself
Creating havoc
I'm sorry if I ever hurt your feelings
It's just that when I want to get my point
across
It's sharper than a dagger so it pierces
through the soul
Of any being that's a factor
I can't help it

Or maybe I can, but I secretly enjoy the
sound of heartbreak
And then I have the audacity to wonder why
Love knocks me on my ass
Then when I fall I fail to focus on the future
because
I'm dwelling on the past
Sometimes I need to cut my tongue off and
place it in my bag
So that when they tell me to hold my tongue
I can whip it out and laugh!
I'm sorry once again
My sarcasm is a thread in my insecurity
blanket
Along with jealousy, stubbornness, and low
self-esteem
Selfishly, I trot down memory lane in a candy
apple red Miata
With leather seats
Drippin' with 20's
Only because I'm 20 and on every birthday I
upgrade and move up an inch
So, down memory lane, I think of all the
times I ever
Hurt another

Ever cursed a mother fucker
Middle finger up saluting the spaceships
Pointed toward the one who cares about me
the greatest
I've come to the conclusion that leaving him
alone
Would be suicide
And he leaving me alone
Would be homicide
Therefore I guess involuntary manslaughter is
within my comfort zone
So excuse me, I still need to borrow
someone's floaty
Before my emotional waves engulf and
Eventually control me

Therapy Blues

I just want to bask in this feeling that I feel
Really feeling seen and heard
Without the confusion about if it's real
Or if someone is a wolf in sheep's clothing
Waiting to pounce on who I think I am
This crush I have, although a manifestation of
Unformed hopes and dreams
Is offering me an opportunity to feel
What it's like to have wings
I fantasize about what could be
With the one I see every week
I do what I am told
Because of my innate need to please
But what if I'm told to love myself more than
someone else?
What of that? Is that a joke?
You mean, I was always enough and worthy?
Just had to be awoke?
That we all are just human magnets
Who attract and repel
There are levels to dysfunction
And there are levels to health?
Levels to which we can measure our

orientations to Self
And depending on where we're at
Is who we'll attract
And be attracted to
Oh, in the midst of transference
My therapy blues.

www.ingramcontent.com/pod-product-compliance
Lightning Source LLC
Chambersburg PA
CBHW072047150726
47996CB00015B/1998